How the

Sitting in the hospital after having two ～ surgeries for my seizures, I realized that I had two choices. Would I live the rest of my life regretting the decisions that I've made, or would I make a choice to live gratefully, accepting all that I have and all that I am? It took some time, but I made myself a promise to live each day with a smile, and love in my heart, and to this day I have not regretted a single moment.

We all say things, but do we make an effort to follow through on what we say? Most often the answer to this question is no, and that is because we either get caught up in doing something else, or we use the excuse that we just don't have the time. The reality is we always have the time; there are 160 hours in a week; we have PLENTY OF TIME; YOU just have to be willing to make the PROMISE to yourself that all that you say will be done, and DO IT!

When you choose to make a PROMISE to YOURSELF, you are making a substantial effort to do the things necessary to work towards being your best, trying your best, and doing your best. You are sending a message out to the universe loud and clear that I AM capable of doing anything, and I AM able to handle all that life throws at me.

Throughout these pages, you will find 31 promises to help you reignite your passion, love your life, and regain your hope. I will make the promises; the key is for you to focus on them and use them. In this updated edition I have made room for you to write your own promises, I encourage you to do so.

**Promise 1: Happiness**

Happiness doesn't depend on the situation you are in, the way your room is set, or in the way your bed is made in the morning. True happiness depends on how your mind is arranged.

Today I promise to be happy because without happiness there are tears, I will focus on all the good in this day and every day, and carry it with me wherever I may go.

**Promise 2: Smile**

A smile is like a ray of sunshine living underneath a cloud of darkness. Share yours.

Your smile brightens not only your world, but everyone else's world around you.

Today I promise to smile and to offer a smile to those who need one. I know that by doing this I will make somebody else's day a lot brighter, and with that, so will mine.

## Promise 3: Choose Love and Let it Lead the Way

Love yourself and all that you have; for that will open the door to everything that you've ever wanted. Say that you love yourself, mean that you love yourself, but most of all, want that love for yourself.

Today I promise to choose love. I will love myself, and I will show loving kindness to others; knowing that with this renewed sense of love I will be able to break through boundaries I never thought possible.

## Promise 4: Appreciation

All that you have, appreciate it. Too often we take things for granted. We forget that all things, big and small, are miracles, and should be looked at that way, including ourselves.

Today I promise to appreciate all that is around me; I will walk around today looking at everything that surrounds me, and take none of it for granted. The trees, sun and the birds were all put here for a reason, and so was I.

**Promise 5: Let Go**

When you let go of what is bringing you down and holding you back, you are allowing yourself the freedom to live a more peaceful life. There is no reason to hold on to worry, heartache, resentment, and pain. Let go, and let more freedom, happiness, and harmony enter your daily life.

Today I promise to let go of all that has been holding me back, bringing me down, and destroying my life. I am ready to live my life with more love, and more peace, and I know that letting go of negativity will allow me to do that.

**Promise 6: Gratitude**

When we are grateful, great things happen. Gratitude is not just a feeling; it is an attitude: An attitude towards life, an attitude towards love, and most of all an attitude towards yourself. It is about seeing the good in not just the big, but the small things as well.

Today I promise to be grateful for all the things that I have, and for all the things that I do not have. I will wake up every morning with a smile, and be grateful for the fact that I am given another day to share with others.

## Promise 7: Acceptance

While it is said that gratitude is one of the greatest gifts you can give yourself, acceptance of your reality is quite possibly the greatest gift of them all. Accept everything that you have, regardless of how tough it may be to accept it. You were given this life and these situations that you are going through for a reason; why fight them? Accept them and move forward to a life of happiness and love, not only for yourself, but for others as well.

Today I promise to accept my reality I will love all that I am, on the inside and out. I will look in the mirror and acknowledge all of my imperfections and know that I am this way for a reason. I will also realize that I am unique, and possibly a little weird, but that's okay, because these two things make me who I am, and I AM beautiful.

**Promise 8: Never give up**

We all have setbacks; they are a part of life. It is how we deal with these setbacks will determine how our lives will unfold. We all make mistakes; we all fail, it's how we choose to look at those mistakes and failures that will ultimately lead us down the road to victory.

Today I promise never to give up. In life I have setbacks, but it is those setbacks that will make me a stronger person. Today I will remind myself that setbacks are a setup for a greater comeback. I was given this life for a reason, and the reason was to succeed and to fail, but NEVER to QUIT!

**Promise 9: Fear**

Fear. It's real. It's what makes us human. When we choose to let fear mold us instead of folding us, life becomes a lot less scary.

Today I promise not to let the presence of fear fold me. Instead, I will embrace my fear with an open heart and conscious mind, allowing my fears to mold me into the person I am willing to become.

**Promise 10: Believe**

Every thought we have is just that, a thought. Whether your thoughts are positive or negative, they are still just thoughts. The only true way for thoughts to come to life is by believing in them Believe in the positive, and positive things will happen; believe in the negative, and negative things will happen.

Today I promise to believe in all the positive thoughts flowing inside of me. I will know that my thoughts are things and the only way for them to take shape, and ultimately for me to live the life that I have been striving for is to BELIEVE. If only negative thoughts are flowing through me, I will acknowledge those negative thoughts, but I will not let them shape who I am because ultimately believing in myself and letting that belief create my thoughts will pave the way for a brighter future ahead of me.

**Promise 11: Laughter**

Laughter is perhaps the best medicine your health care provider can't provide. It increases the feel-good hormones, relieves stress and reduces pain.

Today I promise to laugh. I will laugh at myself, read a good comic, or listen to a good joke. Laughter is the greatest medicine, and I know that by allowing myself to incorporate more of it into my daily life, I will be a much happier, healthier person.

Question:

What did the digital clock say to its mother?

Answer:

Look, ma, no hands!

**Promise 12: Emotions**

There are hundreds of emotions, all of which play a crucial role in how we choose to handle what life throws at us. Most often we choose to hide from our emotions; Stop. Embrace every emotion, feeling it with your heart and soul. Feeling each emotion will allow you to move away from disharmony, and migrate closer to the harmonious life that you are striving to have.

Today I promise to embrace all of my emotions with an open heart. I will feel each emotion wholeheartedly, and not run from them. I will know that feeling the pain, the fear, the happiness and the joy will let me lead a more harmonious life.

**Promise 13: Hate**

Hate is a strong word that takes on many sizes, many shapes, and is all too present in this world. It causes heartache and disharmony in the whole community, or just one individual. Bottom line: it must be stopped.

Today I promise not to hate. I will approach life with a loving heart, and with no judgment, and I will treat others as I would like to be treated. I will remind myself that hate is everywhere, and I too am subject to it, but I will not let it stop me from moving forward.

**Promise 14: Doubt**

You are on the verge of something great, and then you get that feeling deep down in the pit of your stomach. You start to think, "What is this?" It's the voice of doubt; a voice that doesn't want you to move forward but that's not you. YOU want to move forward; YOU want to do great things. The amazing thing is that YOU CAN! Change the channel and tune into the positive voice, and let that positive voice propel you forward towards a more confident and fulfilling life.

Today I promise to be more confident with my inner voice. I will not let the voice of doubt stop me from living the life I have dreamed, or keep me from doing something great. If doubtful thoughts arise, I will acknowledge them, but I will not hold onto them. I am confident, and I will continue to be.

**Promise 15: Dream**

A dream isn't met until we follow through on it. Never lose sight and always strive to do your best in the quest to make it come true. Get obsessed with your dream, show it all the love in the world, and slowly watch the dream blossom. But first, before all else, make yourself a solid promise that YOU will make this happen.

Today I promise to dream big. Even though I might hit a few bumps in the road along the way, and that dream might look distant, I will hold it close to my heart and never lose sight of it. I will have the passion, desire, and drive to do anything, and I will always strive to do my best to get what I want in life.

**Promise 16: Inner Beauty**

There are a lot of beautiful people out there; on the inside. Does this really make them beautiful? Maybe it does, but most often it doesn't. True beauty lies on the inside, and when we choose to open our eyes to see it, our vision of the people around us can change forever. Inner beauty is beautiful. Period. This also holds true for ourselves. Look in the mirror, open your eyes and see all of YOUR imperfections, for those are what make you beautiful. too.

Today I promise to see the inner beauty of the people I come in contact with. I will take the time to know everyone; regardless of appearance or illness or disability, because it is what is on the inside that counts. Inner beauty is beautiful, and I will notice it.

**Promise 17: Listen with Your Heart**

Have you ever felt that no one was listening to you? Whether it be a friend or a loved one; when we choose to listen with our hearts it doesn't only make them feel good, but you as well.

Today I promise to listen with my whole heart. When someone speaks to me. I will listen with both ears, and let there be silence when silence is due; making sure for others to express their needs completely and without hesitation. I will let them finish an entire sentence, and repeat back to them the things that were most important; because in the end I know that will make that person feel not only important, but will also strengthen the bond we have together.

**Promise 18: Life's Too Short**

Life is too short to let anything get in the way of you being happy. We all have tough times; we all cry, we all scream, and we get mad, all for what; to let it rob you of your happy life? No way!

Today I promise to embrace life. I will love more deeply than I ever have before, expect miracles, and embrace them when they come to me. I will also stop fighting with my emotions, for they are a part of life, not an end to it. Life is short. Love deeply, laugh often and regret nothing.

## Promise 19: Say What You Need to Say

In life, there are sometimes things that are left unsaid; say them. You may not have the chance to repeat them. Hold nothing back, and always speak from your heart.

Today I promise to say what I need to say. I will say I love you without hesitation; you are beautiful, just because, and you make me smile with your smile. Say everything, hold back nothing, and let love push you in the right direction.

**Promise 20: Trust**

*The more you trust your intuition, the more empowered you become, the stronger you become, and the happier you become.*

-Gisele Bundchen on the universe

Today I promise to trust myself. Every decision I make today has been made with a true purpose behind it. I am following my heart, and my heart is always right. By trusting my intuition, I am letting my faith in the universe take me by the hand and lead me in the right direction.

## Promise 21: Regret Nothing

All things that we say and do are often done with a purpose, heart, and the right intention. Even if it was the wrong thing, take it and learn from it, and use it as a lesson to better prepare yourself for next time, but never regret it.

Today I promise not to regret anything I've said or done. All the things that I say or do are done with my heart, and I know that my heart is always right. If I made a mistake, I would learn from that mistake, but never regret it; because I know that if I do I am not only stopping myself from moving forward, but I am also living a lie. Say what you mean, do what you do, and never lie to yourself.

**Promise 22: Allow the Abundance to Fill Your Life**

Everything in life is energy, and we all have the choice to choose the right energy to surround ourselves with, there are times in our lives, though that we have a bad day, or get into an argument with a loved one, and that abundant, positive energy flips around to a negative state. We begin to think negative thoughts, or start feeling unhappy, and slowly we start drawing more of that negative energy towards us, and that unhappiness in our hearts deepens even further, not allowing it to open up to new joy, and pleasures of the day. You can change this, though.

Today I promise to open myself up to all things positive and beautiful. I will realize that life is a beautiful mess, and that even when problems arise I will not allow those external circumstances control my internal peace. I will move forward with love in my heart, allowing for new energies to flow, and new abundance to arise.

**Promise 23: Forgive**

When you make an effort to forgive all the people in your life, and you let go of all of the hatred in your heart for those people, true healing can begin.

Today I promise to forgive those that have hurt me, in the past and the present. I will choose to know that forgiveness is the best way to free my mind of any grudges that I may be holding against anyone, and acknowledge that at the same time I am freeing myself from any hate, hurt or pain that I have kept inside of me.

**Promise 24: Don't Play Victim to Your Thoughts**

Our thoughts are things, and they can either drive us to do the most amazing things or just stop in the middle of our tracks and not take a single step forward.  Our thoughts can make us feel miserable, they can make us feel down, or they can continue to make us feel unworthy of everything that we are worthy of. They can also make us feel happy, joyful, and full of love; the choice is yours.

Today I promise not to allow myself to play victim to my thoughts. I will move forward, think positively, and live my life with a grateful heart.

**Promise 25: Self-Care**

You love what you do. It is everything that you have ever dreamed of doing. Why stop now? You have that big test coming up. Why close your eyes to get some sleep? You got sick. Why rest? You see what I am getting at, right? Take a step back, center, reset, and move forward. You will see your progress increase tenfold.

Today I promise to show myself a little self-care. I will unplug from my business for the day and do something special. I will stop obsessing over being perfect in school, and rest my mind. If I know that I am sick, I will not push myself because I know that that will only make things worse. I will stop, center, and breathe my way to success.

**Promise 26: Honesty**

*Honesty and integrity are essential to be successful in life- in all areas of life. The really good news is that anyone can develop both honest and integrity*

-Zig Ziglar

Today I promise to be honest with myself and others. I will be open with the people that I care about most, expressing my true feelings, and holding nothing back. Because in the end, I know that this will not only settle any fear that they may have, but it will also calm my fears as well.

## Promise 27: Cherish Family

*Family is not the most important thing. Family is everything.*

-Michael J. Fox

Today I promise to cherish family. I will give them a call if I am far, a hug when I am near, and make time to listen and be close to them no matter what my day holds in store. Families may not always be close, but in the end, families are the only thing we have. Make time for yours. Work through the rough spots, and hold all of the good times close to your heart.

**Promise 28: Patience**

You know the saying patience is a virtue? It truly is. When we are impatient, our thought process becomes diluted, and we lose focus on what's most important our own inner peace.

Today I promise to be patient with myself and others. I will not let any external situations or inward circumstances create any disharmony in my mind, body, and soul. I will also let the people I come in contact with speak; and I will listen not allowing myself to get upset or frustrated because, in the end, I know that my inner peace is most important to me.

**Promise 29: Courage**

Courage is a thing that lets you know even though things may be scary, everything will work out in the end. Open your heart, clear your mind, keep your focus, and let your courage lead you down the path of abundant victory and healing.

Today I promise to embrace courage. When I am afraid I will remind myself that I AM strong, and that I AM brave, and that I AM resilient, looking my fears in the face with a smile, and a heart wide open; ready to take on anything that comes at me.

**Promise 30: Thank You**

A thank you is a universal expression of gratitude to say that you appreciate all that has been given to you, and all that you have, and all of the people in your life. Too often we neglect to say it to others, but today that changes.

Today I promise to say thank you to everyone that had done a good deed for me, been there for me, been there by my side when I needed it most, and listened to me when no one else would. I will also be thankful for the simplest things, those things that most often go unnoticed, but are the most beautiful things to be thankful for. I will be thankful for them all.

## Promise 31: Keep All Promises

A promise is a bond that you make between yourself and someone else. It solidifies something of importance, and carries with it all of the honesty, trust, and commitment that the person who made it genuinely holds within themselves.

Today I promise to keep my promises, I know that my word is my bond, and when I say something to someone, I will do my best to keep it. In the end, this will not only make me feel comfortable, but will instill a sense of trust in those I made the promise to as well.

*The promise given was a necessity of the past: The word broken is a necessity of the present.*

-Niccolo Machiavelli

I hope that you use these promises to keep on keeping on, in times of darkness, in times of fear, and in times of lost hopes, and allow them to light your path along the way to new healing, and greater focus for a happier, more grateful life.

And with each of your own promises I hope that you allow yourself to create a new vision, a new dream, new hopes, new joy, and a new love for yourself.


Much Love and Gratitude,
Danny Cohen


**Sign up for a FREE five-day greatness through gratitude experience at**

www.keeponkeepingonnow.com

**Follow me on Instagram @Keepitpositivenow**

**Find me on Facebook @ facebook.com/keeponkeepingonnow**


This is your chance to write your own Promises. Listen with your heart and just write. Allow yourself the permission to feel the love, gratitude, and peace in your soul.


Use this space for your own journaling, and allow your soul to open up to new visions, new blessings, new abundance and new hopes.

# Today I promise to:

_____

_____

_____

_____

_____

_____

_____

_____

_____

_____

_____

_____

_____

_____

# Today I promise to:

_____

_____

_____

_____

_____

_____

_____

_____

_____

_____

_____

_____

_____

# Today I promise to:

_____

_____

_____

_____

_____

_____

_____

_____

_____

_____

_____

_____

_____

_____

# Today I promise to:

_____

_____

_____

_____

_____

_____

_____

_____

_____

_____

_____

_____

_____

# Today I promise to:

_____

_____

_____

_____

_____

_____

_____

_____

_____

_____

_____

_____

_____

_____

# Today I promise to:

_____

_____

_____

_____

_____

_____

_____

_____

_____

_____

_____

_____

_____

_____

_____

# Today I promise to:

_____

_____

_____

_____

_____

_____

_____

_____

_____

_____

_____

_____

_____

_____

_____

# Today I promise to:

_____

_____

_____

_____

_____

_____

_____

_____

_____

_____

_____

_____

_____

_____

_____

# Today I promise to:

_____

_____

_____

_____

_____

_____

_____

_____

_____

_____

_____

_____

_____

_____

# Today I promise to:

_____

_____

_____

_____

_____

_____

_____

_____

_____

_____

_____

_____

_____

_____

_____

# Today I promise to:

_____

_____

_____

_____

_____

_____

_____

_____

_____

_____

_____

_____

_____

_____

# Today I promise to:

_____

_____

_____

_____

_____

_____

_____

_____

_____

_____

_____

_____

_____

_____

_____

# Today I promise to:

_____

_____

_____

_____

_____

_____

_____

_____

_____

_____

_____

_____

_____

_____

# Today I promise to:

_____

_____

_____

_____

_____

_____

_____

_____

_____

_____

_____

_____

_____

_____

_____

# Today I promise to:

_____

_____

_____

_____

_____

_____

_____

_____

_____

_____

_____

_____

_____

_____

_____

_____

# Today I promise to:

_____

_____

_____

_____

_____

_____

_____

_____

_____

_____

_____

_____

_____

_____

# Today I promise to:

_____

_____

_____

_____

_____

_____

_____

_____

_____

_____

_____

_____

_____

_____

_____

_____

# Today I promise to:

_____

_____

_____

_____

_____

_____

_____

_____

_____

_____

_____

_____

_____

_____

_____

# Today I promise to:

_____

_____

_____

_____

_____

_____

_____

_____

_____

_____

_____

_____

_____

_____

_____

_____

Made in the USA
Lexington, KY
23 October 2017